The Most Endangered ANIMALS IN THE WORLD

by Tammy Gagne

CAPSTONE PRESS
a capstone imprint

First Facts are published by Capstone Press,
1710 Roe Crest Drive, North Mankato, Minnesota 56003
www.capstonepub.com

Library of Congress Cataloging-in-Publication Data
Gagne, Tammy, author.
The most endangered animals in the world / by Tammy Gagne.
pages cm.—(First facts. All about animals)
Summary: "Interesting facts, colorful photographs, and simple text introduce readers to the
world's most endangered animals"—Provided by publisher.
Audience: Ages 6-9.
Audience: K to grade 3.
Includes bibliographical references and index.
ISBN 978-1-4914-2051-5 (library binding)
ISBN 978-1-4914-2237-3 (paperback)
ISBN 978-1-4914-2257-1 (eBook pdf)
1. Endangered species—Juvenile literature. 2. Rare animals—Juvenile literature. I. Title.
QL83.G34 2015
591.68—dc23   2014032054

Editorial Credits
Kathryn Clay, editor; Bobbie Nuytten, designer; Jo Miller, media researcher; Kathy
McColley, production specialist

Photo Credits
Corel, cover (bottom right); Getty Images: National Geographic/Roy Toft, 9, 22; Newscom:
Design Pics/Dave Fleetham, 17, 22, VWPics/Francois Gohier, 7, 22, ZUMA Press/Photoshot/
Evolve, 5, 22; Shutterstock: Bakalusha, 6, Bildagentur Zoonar GmbH, 15, 22, FloridaStock,
4, guentermanaus, 10, Jean-Edouard Rozey, cover (bottom left), Kletr, 16, Matt Gibson, 11,
22, Monika Hrdinova, cover (top), 1, 22, Photodynamic, 13, Slateterreno, cover (middle),
wormig, 22 (map); SuperStock: John Warburton Lee, 19, 22, Minden Pictures, 21, 22

Printed and bound in China.   5070

Table of Contents

Animals in Danger

Animals around the world are in great danger. One reason is because people have taken over the land these animals call home. Without space to find food or shelter, animals may become **endangered**. Other factors include **pollution**, disease, and the overhunting of a **species**.

endangered—at risk of dying out

pollution—harmful materials that damage the air, water, and soil

species—a group of plants or animals that share common characteristics

4

Fact: Red wolves are just one type of endangered animal. They once roamed the southern part of the United States. Today only about 100 red wolves live in the wild.

North Atlantic Right Whale

North Atlantic right whales are among the rarest sea creatures in the world. Killing this species is illegal today. But many whales die when they get caught in fishing nets. Others die when they run into ships. With only 350 still living, the species may soon become **extinct**.

extinct—no longer existing; an extinct animal is one that has died out, with no more of its kind

Fact: North Atlantic right whale babies are called calves. They measure 13 to 15 feet (4 to 4.5 meters) when they are born.

Pygmy Raccoon

Pygmy raccoons look similar to other raccoons, but they are smaller and have golden tails. This species is found only on the island of Cozumel off Mexico's southeastern coast. Illness is among the top threats to their survival. Stray cats and dogs have brought deadly diseases such as **rabies** to the island. Fewer than 500 pygmy raccoons are left in the wild.

rabies—a deadly disease that people and animals can get from the bite of an infected animal

Fact: Pygmy raccoons are also called Cozumel raccoons and dwarf raccoons.

Jaguar

The jaguar has lost much of its **habitat** over time. People have cut down the forests where these large cats live. Hunting has also decreased their numbers. The species used to live in both the southwestern United States and Central and South America. About 15,000 jaguars are left today, mostly in South America.

habitat—the natural place and conditions in which an animal or plant lives

Fact: The jaguar is the third largest cat in the world today. Only the tiger and lion are larger.

Mountain Gorilla

About 700 mountain gorillas live in central Africa today. Many others have been the victims of hunting and human wars. Ongoing fighting in Rwanda, Uganda, and the Congo makes saving the species especially difficult. Hunting mountain gorillas is illegal. But **poachers** continue to kill these animals.

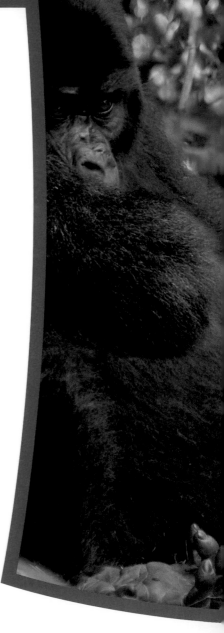

poacher—someone who hunts or fishes illegally

Fact: Baby mountain gorillas ride on their mothers' backs after they are about 4 months old. They continue riding up to age 3.

Northern Sportive Lemur

The northern sportive lemur is the most endangered lemur in Madagascar. Only about 20 of these animals live on the island today. Slash-and-burn farming has caused their habitat to shrink. This practice of burning land is thought to make the soil richer. But it destroys the homes of many animals.

Fact: About 100 different lemur species live in Madagascar. Like the northern sportive lemur, many of them are endangered.

Hawaiian Monk Seal

About 1,100 Hawaiian monk seals are left in the wild. Many are killed when they get caught in fishing nets. But some members of this endangered species are being killed by their own kind. Scientists have discovered that groups of males sometimes attack females. This practice is called mobbing.

Fact: Hawaiian monk seals do not fear people like many other wild animals do. They will not flee when a person approaches them.

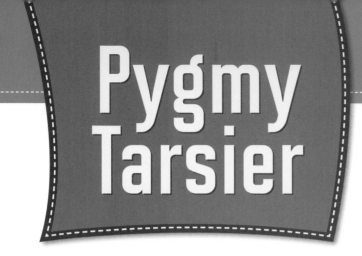

Pygmy Tarsier

Too much attention can be a bad thing. This is the case with the pygmy tarsier in Indonesia. Tourists are drawn to this endangered species. But when people get too close, these animals become extremely tense. As a result they will often bang their heads so hard they kill themselves. To protect the tarsiers, tourists are now taught to stay away from the animals.

Fact: For more than 80 years, the pygmy tarsier was thought to be extinct. But in 2008 members of the species were found again on an island in Indonesia.

Kakapo Parrot

The kakapo parrot from New Zealand is the only parrot that cannot fly. Cats and rats have hunted this unique species to near extinction. Because it cannot fly, this species has a hard time getting away from **predators**. Fewer than 150 kakapo parrots are left in the wild today. Members of the Kakapo Recovery Program and other groups work to increase the populations of this endangered species.

predator—an animal that hunts other animals for food

Fact: So few kakapo parrots exist that researchers have given almost all of them names.

Range Map

	North Atlantic Right Whale
	Hawaiian Monk Seal
	Red Wolf
	Pygmy Raccoon

	Northern Sportive Lemur
	Kakapo Parrot
	Pygmy Tarsier
	Jaguar
	Mountain Gorilla

Glossary

endangered (in-DAYN-juhrd)—at risk of dying out

extinct (ik-STINGKT)—no longer existing; an extinct animal is one that has died out, with no more of its kind

habitat (HAB-uh-tat)—the natural place and conditions in which an animal or plant lives

poacher (POH-chur)—someone who hunts or fishes illegally

pollution (puh-LOO-shuhn)—harmful materials that damage the air, water, and soil

predator (PRED-uh-tur)—an animal that hunts other animals for food

rabies (RAY-beez)—a deadly disease that people and animals can get from the bite of an infected animal

species (SPEE-sheez)—a group of plants or animals that share common characteristics

Critical Thinking Using the Common Core

1. How do pygmy raccoons differ from other raccoons? (Key Ideas and Details)

2. Reread page 4 about how animals become endangered. What can people do to keep animals from becoming endangered? (Integration of Knowledge and Ideas)

Read More

Boothroyd, Jennifer. *Endangered and Extinct Mammals*. Animals in Danger. Minneapolis: Lerner, 2014.

Hoare, Ben. *Endangered Animals*. DK Eyewitness Books. New York: DK Publishing, 2010.

Orr, Tamra B. *Battling Extinction*. Follow the Clues. Ann Arbor, Mich.: Cherry Lake Publishing, 2014.

Internet Sites

FactHound offers a safe, fun way to find Internet sites related to this book. All of the sites on FactHound have been researched by our staff.

Here's all you do:
Visit *www.facthound.com*
Type in this code: 9781491420515

 Check out projects, games and lots more at **www.capstonekids.com**

Index